Terra Infirma

Terra Infirma

Poems by Carol Westberg

David Robert Books

Published by David Robert Books
P.O. Box 541106
Cincinnati, OH 45254-1106

Cover photograph © Lia Rothstein
Cover design by Joanna Bodenweber

ISBN: 9781625491336
LCCN: 2015938341

Poetry Editor: Kevin Walzer
Business Editor: Lori Jareo

Visit us on the web at www.davidrobertbooks.com

Acknowledgments

With appreciation to the editors of the journals in which the following poems first appeared:

"Tyranny of Dreams," originally published in *CALYX, A Journal of Art and Literature by Women*, Vol. 26, No. 3, 2011.

"Yellow Door in Open Field," published in *Salamander*, Fall–Winter 2013-2014.

"Driving West at Sunset," published in *North American Review*, Spring 2014.

"Epiphytes" published in the spring 2014 *DMQ Review* and "We Pass Like Thieves" published in the spring 2015 *DMQ Review*.

"Entwined" and "Next Time" published in *The Café Review*, Winter 2010.

"The Disruptive Power of Pigs" and "Invisible Hand" (first published under the title "Vortex") originally published in *OVS Magazine*, Winter 2010.

"The Disruptive Power of Pigs" was also selected for display in a downtown store window as part of the Keene Literary Festival in September 2012.

Thank you also to the editors who selected *Terra Infirma* as a finalist for the 2014 Tampa Review Prize for Poetry.

Vermont Law School invited me to read "Intelligent Life" (under the title "Beyond SoRo") as part of its 2011 commencement ceremony.

Deep gratitude to Sue Burton, Clyde Watson, Pam Harrison, Laura Foley, Heather Bagley, Lisa Russ Spaar, and my husband, Peter Travis, for careful listening and reading, wise suggestions, and telling the truth.

To the memory of
Craig Stephen Westberg

Contents

3

1

Who pierced the heart of time?
— Antonio Machado

Swamp Walk

In the body, out of it,
    I walk sadness away
past the infinitesimal span of the sand flea,
    of the white bird out of sight.
Striations of dusky bark
    pierce my caged heart.
What's that buzzing under
    the canopy of white cedar in the swamp?
Soon it will be time to go.
    Under skin soft as a heartbeat
the body carries me
    from swamp to shore. Cliffs crumble
to sand before my unseeing eyes.
    My ears barely hear wingbeats,
knives sharpening in salt air.
    Don't wait for me,
my shoulders shaped to the weight of silence.
    Out of the body, I let grief be,
fly to the edge of the cliff
    disintegrating in its own time.
In the body, out and in again
    to the walk's end.

In Time's Maw

Careful what you ask for, like time.
    Always too little or too much.
How do you like it now?
    And now? Weekends disappear
into a sameness of days. March seeps away
    with the cat teaching me to sleep
in daytime, our conversations languid, spare.
    It's not how you sleep,
but how much of the dream remains.
    The garden hose looms, unattached
two feet from thirsting grass.
    I try to meditate on Caravaggio's angel,
on his shining black and white wings.
    How did he get those robes on and off?
What would you like to do today,
    nothing? Is that *nothing* like a monk
or *nothing* like a woman who lost
    her job and watches prime time all day?
God waits in the park, on the bus.
    What happens when you sit
and expect nothing, do nothing but breathe?
    Poetry might be a reason for being
or riding around hoping to run into
    the perfect place for lunch. Here comes
one of those words I have to look up
    again like *mimetic* or *eponymous.*
Can I step off the bus anywhere
    and still get back on?

Breech

From the moment of my feet-first birth
I've borne witness to accidents
and random acts praised as free will.

Someone paved over the forests of my childhood—
words will not save you now, missy!
Truck tires buzz on the freeway as I imbibe

silence in the cicada songs inaudible to our species.
We outlast elation and despair,
having learned to live forward and back at the same time.

On the downside of my century, I sleep fitfully,
wake at the cycle's midpoint, and expend
some minutes upside down

pondering a new color for the front door.
Marry me and my grief becomes yours, also my joy.
In the end I choose to begin again.

Invisible Hand

From an antebellum brick house,
a child gazed out French windows
toward a pond. As she half-

watched, still water began
to spiral down just off-center as though
an invisible hand had pulled a plug.

The girl flew out the side door
in time to see lilies and turtles swirl slowly
out of sight, their tranquil world

sucked into a vortex, sliding
from daylight to dark, from upper air
into the earth.

Next morning the pond was gone—
pollywogs, minnows, and hydra lost
to an underworld of sludge,

subterranean byways mingling poisons
from old tires, bed-frames, and stoves
tossed year after year down other sinkholes

opening without warning across Todd County.
Years later the woman returns
to her childhood home, where dogwood

opens earlier each spring. At the far end
of the garden, she buries her father,
mother, and husband in turn.

Under her red Kentucky earth
plates may shift as she serves visitors
iced tea with mint sprigs.

Any day a new hole may open,
take sheep, her three Tennessee Walkers,
her whole house down.

Hurricane Flats

Shouts sweep down the swollen river
as a cow passes under the Chelsea Street Bridge.
Does she hear the weird music of boulders
rolling beneath the surface?
In the storm's wake, flattened trees
angle downstream along the riverbank, roots
exposed as brown waters recede.
Small animals seek dry places,
and survivors blink into surreal sunshine,
despair on the rise. Thick ecumenical
mud covers crops, playing fields, family photos.
The eyes of rats in his basement
shine in the farmer's dreams.

Bone Flute

In those days my child lived in me
until she slipped the placenta
and spoke in tongues beyond my grasp.

What's that sound coming out of the dahlias?
It's not what you say but how,
Mother chanted from the grass, never easy
in the bones that flexed to release
each child in turn.

Songs rise from the hollows,
from the bones of villains and saints.

We fill up with love, rage,
love again as the light hums
and the dark hums. Daughters, Mother,
unruly multitudes I didn't choose—
they inhabit each song.

Driving West at Sunset

From the back seat Mother murmurs,
You didn't get the windshield clean.

My daughter, thirteen, dozes off beside her,
unaware of the sun infusing this road with gold.

Rows of young corn and beans slide by
the side window. Near ones speed past in a blur,

layer by layer slanting more slowly
toward the horizon. Such fields so free of weeds

must make these neighbors proud.
Close-mown lawns surround each farmhouse,

sentinels from a life I fled at first chance.
In the driver's seat, thinking I'm the only one awake,

I reach over to touch my father's hand,
at rest on his left knee, a farmer's hand gone soft,

its ropy veins swollen. The gold ring
cuts into his finger like a wire grown year

by year more embedded in a tree.
In a swift move his right hand captures mine,

and we drive a few miles in this proximity.
What binds us rides along unspoken.

Channeling

I was just channeling my mother
and thought I'd criticize the soup. Happiness bubbles up

to think I belong to a tribe of mothers who watch
over the pot for daughters about to consume

carrots, leeks, and cream. Adjust the pepper and the salt.
How far does the chicken graze from the roost?

Inside I carry a woman who places spoons with care,
accepts the weight of the water in the pail, gets down

on hands and knees to scrub the woodwork clean.
I can still channel Mother's power to hurt most

the ones she loves best, her silent fear
there is no *there* inside, also her love of bittersweet.

I taste for cumin and lime as soup simmers in the pot,
brims over my blue ceramic spoon.

Seals Do Not Come When Called

Good for the seals and selkies
swimming in their mythic element.

Good for my daughters,
who do not always come when called.

Swim on, selkies and daughters,
as tides rise and fall, as these languid

summer days ebb away. In today's high waves
thick with silt and seaweed churned up

in last night's storm, a harbor seal surfaces
not far from shore, eyes me,

and in her own time slides under.

Scrabble Lesson

My daughter eyes a triple-letter square,
pleads wordlessly until
I abandon *levity*, spell out *viral*
in a less auspicious place.
Aunt Clary, a master at eighty-three,
smacks down *mug* above
the coveted space. The child sulks
in her chair. *Stick around,*
says Clary. *It just gets worse.*

Wisdom in the Fox's Eye

Crayfish, earthworm, mandrake root
under and in the lucent air.

My younger daughter watches
an unnamed city burn on TV, does not yet see

how such fire might touch her, nor flood,
earthquake, the charred boy of her dreams.

She will embrace love and hunger,
fear and the root of her fear. The crystal twists

on its thinning chain in the window, making
vibrations that might send her to Rio or Beiruit.

Everything seems possible under a new moon
that illuminates her back yard in March.

Let the Fire Fall

Father started the Firefall in 1872 when he
pushed his campfire over the Glacier Point cliff.
— Fred McCauley

Summers we lived in Yosemite, I thrilled
to the Firefall each night at nine—
flames of red fir cascading off Glacier Point
three thousand feet to the cool Merced.

Under her veil of silence, Mother
chose not to abandon my father, brothers,
and me, leaving our stars aligned.
The natural world continued

to rain fire and water. Storm clouds
careened past our farmhouse
in a triumph of purple ivory blues,
the funnel cloud still aloft. Minutes later

a tornado howled through the next town,
taking one side of the street,
leaving the other intact—those spared
and those not fused into kinship.

I chopped 60 chilies for my wedding sauce,
too hot for some. In the wake
of later damage I call up
the Firefall's extravagant cascade.

The Disruptive Power of Pigs

I take those pigs everywhere
    under the eight layers of my skin—
midwinter sows, piglets attached,
    sad-eyed Mort the boar I ride
out of the feedlot, willing him to sprout wings
    through his white wiry hide.
He likes his straw clean, gates open,
    every itch scratched. Pig nature calls him
to grab the melon rind with his whole mouth.
    My father gives me the runt
to bottle-feed until it can fend for itself.
    Years later, under my azure coat, I carry
that piglet to Istanbul and Paris.
    We visit alabaster geese, go snout
to snout with kin in paintings
    like Bruegel's roasted pig that trots along,
a carving knife slipped under its hide.
    Human nature calls me
to open my mouth and eyes wide. The pig girl
    travels everywhere inside, still wanting,
wanting the melon, the wings.

Radiant Music

My daughter has been coughing up blood
for months and telling no one.

Snow blankets the branches at last,
offering more cover for hibernating life.

I turn up Mahler's Fifth on the radio and am swept
decades back to the story of my aunt's first child.

At 18 months, she bled from her mouth,
ears, and eyes, as fever ignited the white magnolias

outside her window. The child's eyes flew open
just before she died, and she cried out

O beautiful music! I don't speak
to my scientist daughter of this mystery

or of the refuge some take in faith. She calls to say
she's found more blood in her urine.

As we wait to hear from the merciless tests,
I silently rage against indifferent gods

and affirm my belief in music,
each child's life, the sanctity of snow.

Red Grass at Sunrise

Manzanita bark, devil's horn,
amaryllis unfolding, aflame.

A redbird wings past the poplars
humming in a foreign tongue

above the granite bench
where I lie slowly down

silent as a grave marker except for breath
and the shushing of my blood.

Tyranny of Dreams

I don't mean to compete
over whose child suffers more,

yours bleeding hope away each month
or mine signed up for her first

shock treatment. The moon's impassive
over all our children's dreams.

As a mother I know fear
wraps its hands around the throat.

A phone call can turn the night air to ice.
Today a fire burns in the woodstove

and Garrison Keillor jokes on the radio
about SSRIs. I doubt his son ever took a razor

and sliced line by line into his thigh
to silence voices clamoring inside.

But what do I know of his son,
our daughters? They all must strive

to rise each day and find
two comfortable shoes to slip into.

I've grown wary of the tyranny of dreams.
Just now I mean to pad downstairs

for tea and toast that I'll spread thick
with your wild plum jam.

Ode to My Daughter's Horse

You, son of great steeds, carrier of dreams—
carry her into the air and safely down

Praise to your sound legs and hooves
that sweep her over sweet grasses,
over the moon's path shimmering on open water

Praise to your gray coat flecked red
dark as the blood surging inside

Praise also to the fire inside, tempered
by her wise young hands

Praise to the mane she twists in her fingers,
wraps with black thread,
and later clips free

Praise to the strong will and good heart
beating to its mystic end

Praise to the amber eye she gazes into,
window on a kindred soul

You, winner of long races,
listen through your intelligent ears—
carry her, carry her through

Postcard from San Vitale

Take this lion I send you from Ravenna—
big wilderness cat with fiery eyes and mane flourishing
against indigo sky and emerald grass. See
his ribs and claws extend, teeth aglitter, fierce to live.

Take him for a talisman to deliver you from a lunatic moon.
Conjure him on afternoons you feel too woozy to rise.

Take his volition as your own into those desecrated days.
I pray to whatever gods may hear that you not be offered up
like some mystic lamb into the doomed trinity
of suffering, sacrifice, and dreams of a gleaming afterlife.

Take the eagle, too, winged man, and ox
laid tile by tile beside the lion.

Take the power of the octagon, the triangle, and the circle
built into the rust, black, and tan mosaic floor
where I stand speechless
beneath this brilliant, immaculate dome, willing you

to open your eyes and stare down unfathomed distances
like a predator, not prey.

Small Miracle of the Keystone

Roof caved in, stained glass
long gone from the rose,
afternoon light gapes through ravaged windows
in the shell of the Abbey of San Galgano.
I stand in silence on the rough grass,
dwarfed in the shadow of soaring walls.
A Cistercian chant resonates
in my chest eight centuries after
the keystone slipped into place.

In Gubbio

We arrive in this Apennine hill town with no plan
but to wander its maze of narrow streets
with stone houses, thick medieval doors, here
and there on the Via dei Consoli the tongue
of a staircase graced with red geraniums.

You tell me how St. Francis struck a deal
with the black wolf who agreed not to eat the people
of Gubbio or their sheep if they would feed him.
How useful to speak the wolf's language,
to be able to persuade him from his hunger.

On a side street just off the Via del Monte
a round-faced woman motions us inside
to see an exhibit that turns out to be
instruments of torture—rack, wheel, high-backed chair
with leather straps and metal head ring.

I would have told them anything to escape
the turn of that screw, eight-inch nails sinking into
my back. In minutes we flee the claustrophobic room,
leaving a few coins on the flowered plate
set out by the stairway to the second floor.

As we stroll on, unbidden thoughts take me
to other places I hadn't meant to see, where I'm caught
in fascination's grip like a gawker at an accident.
I don't tell you of the deals I see myself making
with the rapacious black wolf inside.

Outside Assisi

Especially for Master Brother Sun
Who illuminates the day for us
— From "The Canticle of the Creatures," St. Francis

After basking in Lorenzetti's Our Lady of Sunset—
Mary gazing into her son's eyes as if they both
know the way, her right thumb gesturing into his future—

we exit the basilica, take a wrong turn
up a cobbled street, and find ourselves trudging outside
the city wall, thinking our road must angle uphill soon,

wind in perhaps through a gate near Rocca Maggiore,
towering above us, above the implacable wall, dusky
olive groves, lavender, and scorched grass.

Outside the wall, we might have savored the Umbrian hills,
tilled fields spanning out below us like a painting,
but we feel anxious about how long our water will last

as the midday sun intensifies, scan the stones for an entry,
not knowing if our road will continue down,
or if we should retrace our steps up to the basilica

to stand and drink in the cool frescos again—
St. Francis with his beasts and birds, his stigmata signifying
he was chosen to illuminate the way.

Vespers in Sant'Apollinare

Not devout in this faith, I lose
all sense of self, could be that single sheep,
bright mosaic white on green,
following no visible path, small head raised
as high above the hand of God emerges
from layers of blue and orange clouds—
to bless? to intervene? to strike?

A mercy, I think, we can't see
our alpha and omega, how
each beginning courses to its end.
My daughters, my lambs, need me every hour,
then not at all. They follow
with trusting eyes as I find and lose my way.
Then they lead me.

I wish they could be here enveloped
in mystery, bathed in this light.
My father called me his little lamb,
neither of us knowing how love transcends.
Not paradise I want but this
spacious sky, wind lifting acanthus leaves,
a dove flying not far behind my living lambs.

Rush Hour

Descend from green-eyed leaves outside the metro
into the tunnel at Saint-Sulpice. Hands to self,
earbuds plugged in, my private apocalypse

in the midst of this press and heave. I dismiss
small bugs of discontent. Summer coming, then fall.
Which crisis is about to arise?

A great star fell to earth, turned the river bitter
as wormwood for many years.

Nothing comes true and it's gone
in a heartbeat. Next stop Cité.
In the infinity of my desires, a new one

overtakes the old. Push me up against the door
till we slide down to all fours.
Four seasons, four horses.

Oh the horses—white,
red, pale, and black as the deathly rider.

If only I could remember
the four noble truths when I need them,
which is now. And now.

Last in, first out. No horizon in view.
Above the surface
everyone talking about the new moon.

On the opening
of the sixth seal, the moon bloomed red as blood.

What could be better than a night sky?
Hand on thigh. Under white sheets, plastic, dirt.
I cast a handful into Mother's grave.

Which of the four winds blew her seed to earth,
and which took my mother away?

Like Yeats, I want a séance, a hand moving
to prove there's more.
I want to believe in the next place.

2

The world is gone. I must carry you.

— Paul Celan

Yellow Door in Open Field

The door in the field is held upright
by my saying so.

Frogs before storm, wind on the rise.
The door opens and I still can't see

what lies on the other side.
I decide like a deer tasting the wind:

one way will be the death of me
as will the other. Smoke in sunrise,

firefly on ice. Should I give my heart
to the open road?

There is no road, no sky to own.
The yellow door remains upright.

Epiphytes

As clouds scuttle across the hardwood floor,
I contemplate exits by fire and flood,
having risen too high to jump without breaking.
*

How will I find the friend within the enemy within?
I lose my way, look askance, admit my terror
of the *fête d'adieu.* Dazzle and repeat.
*

My father bequeathed me his golden chopsticks.
What more could I need? Overwhelm fixes me in bed,
bereft of the memory of my exit strategy.
*

If you don't believe in the afterlife, what do you
attune to, my enemy, my friend? Turned over,
the leaf of despair can resurrect a life.
*

Rinse and repeat. I'll tell you what drives me
through the looking glass. Neotropical,
the epiphyte absorbs what it needs through air.
*

Don't wait for me to emerge from the bark
of the Sequoia. I admit I've slept with the enemy
every night of my life. See what love comes to?
*

Seriously, I'm more afraid of shame
than of the afterlife. In my next life, love reciprocates.
Repeat the tender part, the lick and caress.
*

I expect nothing in return for feeding the birds,
but I want you to take seriously my next exit.
Take it from either side of the leaf.

Questions My Brother Will Not Ask

Was it a morning like any other
biking high in Arizona, setting out early

on the trail, pushing yourself as usual
up and up without respite? As you breathed

in the dry pine air, did you leave
this year's troubles in your wake? Did you feel

the January sun's embrace? After you turned
to head downhill, wheels spinning faster,

did you wish to escape
more than usual as you flew on

gathering speed? Did euphoria overtake
your wish to leave Earth behind?

As you hit that big rock and sailed
head first over the handlebars

into the shocking blue sky, did anyone
in this life dare you to look back?

Halo

You inhale through a hole in your throat
attached to the machine that breathes for you.
A silver halo drilled into your skull

secures your caged body, silent as sand.
They've stitched the cut that gaped
from your mouth into your left cheek. You sleep

as long as the drug drips into your vein, wake
to hear, see, mouth words, unable to escape pain.
It's my turn to see you alone.

How small you look, big brother—
hands still, legs still. I'm afraid to wake you
but touch your shoulder, wrist, foot.

I worry that your swollen feet will get cold
exposed with no sheet, then remember
they can't be a source of pain. Only a miracle

could let you move again below the neck.
How could you not fear this tethered life
more than death? You climbed high into the Andes,

cast your small plane's shadow over ocean
and desert, and just yesterday tore breakneck
down a Mazatzal trail to crash and sever

the lacework of nerves at the top of your spine.
A mercy that you, who don't believe in miracles,
wake able to shape the words *Let me go.*

After your children smuggle in the dog
to lick your face, the hospital sends a slim angel
to turn off the machine.

No Goodbyes, No Regrets

Too late to create space
        for a listening hand, an opening.
I believe you loved me, too,
        brother, though you closed
the last door without farewell, left me
        in this field of grief.
No matter now with you in ashes
        which fears blocked the way.
No regrets, you said.
        I regret our lost hours, years.
This morning the oblivious birds chirp
        for all they're worth.
What does it matter in geologic time?
        We refuse to see even as the veil
falls away. We remember
        what we remember, call it truth.

To My Brother in Ashes

For forty mornings after you died
I sat in silence to invite you in.
Tears arrived but no sign from you.

Today I remember how a friend hovered
at the edge of death on a reed mat
in a clinic outside Bombay.

Close to the ceiling, he looked down
on his body, separate from,
seeing and hearing, unable to speak.

Your body has been burned to ash,
brother, and still I entreat whatever shape
your spirit might take—

bear, dog, or falcon risen from ash.
Or no shape, no voice,
shiver on an evening breeze.

Afloat

Aspen leaf, memory of the leaf
      swept down. I am a stream that carries you
in each season—howling, meandering,
      almost still. Your absence resonates
in my chest, in my throat.
      Only I carry our memories in this world now.
Two children rode bareback between fields
      of greening alfalfa or snow-covered stubble,
explored thick woods on the peninsula
      overgrown with wild plums, built a hideout
between branches of the stream
      that disappeared underground.
We dug a hole just deep enough to crouch in,
      covered it with planks, soil, leaves,
didn't tell our mother we took the striped rug
      from the north room to line our dirt floor.
After luminous hours, we moved on.
      Now everything has come undone, and I go on
sleeping without dreaming, waking, sleeping.
      And I go on picking up leaf after yellow leaf.

No Sequel

The faster the action in the previews,
the more I yearned to sit still,

and more still, to sink inward and escape
the shrieks toe to toe, tongue

to tongue, fist to jaw. Tonight
high-pitched voices seem hard to hear

in this room humming
with conversations between strangers

saying nothing that lodges in my mind.
Sparks from her bronze necklace

distract me from what its wearer
might intend with her story of three dogs.

I remind myself to attend,
to listen transfixed,

as if this woman were my brother,
and these his final words.

Next Time

An eagle, the boy said,
      or a loon. Next time
I might be moss
      or stone or stream.

Quince, Shadow, Crossing

I haunt your bedside, read Neruda out loud,
hold your thin hand with its grip

out of scale like an infant's, recall a photo
of your hand cradling mine.

Your eyelids lift and you seem to see
a stranger. I swab your mouth with water,

watch you receive morphine, hum
a little lullaby, making it up as I go along.

The last thing you asked, three days ago,
was *How far away is home?* You might have seen

the quince tree outside your childhood home,
light or shadow from some place beyond.

A nurse says I can leave to eat—
they will call me in time. But the call comes

after your last breath. Too late, I return
to lay my head on your silent chest.

Did you hold on to cross over in solitude?
Father, I didn't want you to die alone.

May you have slipped gently from this life,
knowing love soars for you.

Gone from your bedside moments before your last
rasp of breath, I was with you to the end.

Black Walnut in a Wooden Bowl

— For Carl Dwight Leland Westberg

Every furrow, gooseberry bush, swarm of bees
     on a sultry day. A thunderhead closing in fast
before the downpour. Each count between the flash
     and crack as fierce wind sweeps over our farm.
Rutted mud in our abandoned lane pressed up
     between bare toes. Every firefly, every slice
of lemon meringue pie. Soft snout of the piglet
     you gave me to feed by hand. Children's tracks
through low drifts between house and barn. Mornings
     at the kitchen table with you reading aloud
to Mother, my brothers, or me. Each golden book,
     like *The Raven*, too huge for me to hold alone.
Digger pinecones you sent years after
     those summers living in Yosemite. Every verse
of "How Much Is That Doggie in the Window?"
     Each granddaughter humming her own song
in the walnut rocker you made for me. Every step,
     patient or not, with your walker. Each
and every time you asked, *How far away is the sea?*

Monsoon Season

Time is the river,
death is the river. Breath ebbs
and ebbs again.

I am underwater mourning
the sudden death of my brother
when my father dies,

and new waves break
over the sorrow
I am suspended in.

Thoughts of one loss
evoke the other
as griefs collide.

Tears for the father,
for the brother—they mingle.
Friends say time heals

but I do not want comfort now.
I float with the river
that sweeps me out to sea.

Low Tide

At low tide everything will be revealed—
spiral shells abandoned
by hermit crabs, a rusted hinge
washed up on a plank,
shining outlines of estuary pools
on the long slope across
the intertidal zone.
Here the last waves break away
as I scan the expanse
of silver-green ridged with white
reflecting a coral sunrise.
Spiny bones land next to a stranded
jellyfish—still life of the rage
that abrades my sorrow.

My Father's Ginkgo Grown Tall

Father boat, Mother sail, I sing to you,
to wind and the Perseids. I sing
            to the space outside
            and in,
to time on its tether
            and never bound,
as you, ghost Father and Mother, left your children
free and linked under the ginkgo, oldest tree.

            On this coast the air stills
            as a gale force gathers in the west.
Last week we flew from sea level
to the San Juans and climbed on foot for miles
            to scatter your first son's ashes
            among pine cones and columbine,
then returned
to the changed place we call home.

Mother boat, Father sail, I praise you
for your tenacity, for holding on
            to land and air,
            to old spirits none can see.
I sing to each generous heart,
to you and all children who carry on,
            each one blood and bone,
air and water, seed and ash.

Into and After

Walkers tethered to their dogs in spring.
        Jazz on the wind. Small stuff,
evil and good, slipping from eel mind.
        The mocked child's terror.
Ranunculus in a clear glass vase on the table.
        Explosion in a crowd
and smoke billowing into the tropopause after.
        Being able to walk.

The Tides Repeat

A wave swallows me whole.
      Mere minnow, a four year old,
I drown in a terrible gasp for air,
      somehow survive the undertow
off Redondo Beach.
      Trembling on a shimmer of sand,
I feel the insatiable ocean
      seethe at my back.

Years slide by,
      and time is all I have, wave
of days I ride, a survivor.
      Taste of salt air,
smell of my newborn's skin,
      whisper of a glistening planet
through a universe
      of minuscule truths.

Dread fills my lungs, smothers
      hope that revives and lives.
Love's tsunami spits me out,
      my voice keening
above the flood, willing each child
      to reach for her one and only life.

Refuge

Far from fault lines and oceans,
      our farm holds the center
of the plains I abandoned years ago.
      Dark topsoil lies fallow under drifts
my brother and I rode through,
      our horses thick with winter.
Bounded by dense timber to the north,
      changing under the keen eyes
of the sparrow hawk, rolling fields
      shaped my sense of horizon,
offered grain and sky and refuge.
      These fields bore the transitory scars
of hooves and feet, of tractor,
      plough, and harrow. I took root
in tamed acres that allowed me to roam.
      Our father dreamed this land
would sustain his people
      for another hundred years,
but his children moved west and east,
      carrying the seeds of our heritage.
We returned to bury our parents' ashes
      in the constant land
and called the auctioneer.
      Today the name on the deed changed,
but no one owns the land that holds me.

White Magnolia

Blossoms splay against the brick wall
petals after snow

the probability of forgiveness rises
when you start small   parking lot trespass

broken glass   not the goblet from Prague
work up to some old harm

fused into your back   your glance
abyss of lines around your mouth

how long   have you cherished
this fixed image   this dirge

and does your burden weigh
less than yesterday   o pliant mind

Quartet for the End of Time   shimmer
of the violin's ascent   diminishing

Air

Surrounding the subject. Being it.
    A box of, a box without.

Terrified gasp of not having.
    High and rarefied, unsullied by lungs.

Companion to fire
    and its many futures on Earth.

Even in dreams of flying
    I persist in my ignorance.

Buoyant at the open window in spring,
    I wave my hand through the invisible.

3

We should insist while there is still time.

— Jack Gilbert

Carrier of Gestures

I carry the music of languages learned
        and lost, the stone streets of Rome,

the Tiber's muddy flow, songs of ancestors
        and small fish. I carry mustard greens, eggplant,

sweet artichokes fried crisp beyond the press
        of a metro sultry with tenderness.

I carry the shrines to Mithra I chanced on
        in Ostia Antica and gestures

of Etruscans alive in each descendant
        who looks me in the eye.

Mortal Wings

Strange angel for the gods to send
to the Villa Farnesina—thin, balding mortal
in his striped shirt and striped tie of purple, green,
mustard, red vivid as the tints of frescos
telling cautionary tales.

I lean back in a chair, gaze up at the ceiling
at the bride's blooming moth wings
in Raphael's *Wedding Banquet of Cupid and Psyche*
when the man asks if I recall the third task
wrathful Venus set for the too-beautiful Psyche.

Between us we tick off the grains, wool, water
from the River Styx, and Psyche's quest to find
the box she won't resist opening.
I half-see the man's bad teeth and trembling hands
as we talk of curiosity, of trials set by jealous gods.

Later in the entryway on this first day of spring,
he tells me it's his last trip to Rome,
does not say how long he expects to tour before
cancer takes him to the river of tears,
carrying cakes for Cerberus, coins for Charon.

He flaps on his ungainly way, leaving me
in the midday sun to contemplate
this stranger's unexpected gift.
How many trials, how many deaths
will it take to wake me?

Cloud Cover

I count on clouds to take me to the heart
of the heart of the matter. How can the meek inherit

the earth if the clamorous won't abandon camp?
Mother's tears fall on the mulberry bush, and I see

I must add water to reconstitute a life, must stop
pleading guilty to crimes we didn't commit.

Outside the restaurant, my daughter on her cell phone
drives off alone, abandoning me *in medias res.*

I stand still at the side of the road, waiting
for the landscape to embrace me bone by bone.

Or I pan for gold at the kitchen sink. Who's to say
I won't find a wedding ring in the dishpan,

speckled trout in clouds? To my great good fortune,
a lustrous sky circumscribes the globe.

Liminal

In this no man's land between
sleep and waking, I act as no one's friend
or enemy but my own.

Insomniac, I croon to my anxieties,
seek a new lullaby
that can ease us all to sleep.

Late afternoon I fight to stay awake
in the warm lull of the freeway,
eyelids heavy as my heart.

Night or day I work maddeningly
against myself. Sages say, *Wake up! Relax!*
Impossible instructions! Here

where earth and sea attract, repulse,
attract, I abide in the ebb and flow
of the habitat between.

Pouring Tea in the Dark

Early morning I pour by sound
from the iron teapot that holds an ocean

Anything might rise from underneath
the surface—all tentacles, all teeth

Secrets I keep even from myself elude shape
but not patterns of flight

A still self returns from the time lapse
of my breath to a sunrise chorus of small birds

The scarlet tanager flies off the poster
on the refrigerator door

Entwined

It can never be satisfied, the mind, never.
— Wallace Stevens

Anxiety shows up tonight in the wrong shoes,
    feet ablaze, her notorious fingers picking at scabs
long vanished from skin once smooth
    as a cat's eye but not from a psyche
so easily swayed by rumor of storm, wasps,
    lurid flames from neighbors or strangers.
Tonight I sleep but fitfully, waking to *3:00 a.m.*
    glowing fluorescent green. How long, I
wonder, will books be made of paper, glue, and ink?
    Rumi, Carson, Augustine, Cortazar—
my collection breathes no place else in the universe.
    Not even I want to hum my litany
of fears, hopes, and undone chores to kindred souls
    who still can't read themselves to sleep.

On Limantour

On this rough coast stones whisper
in a bitter breeze over Earth's thin crust
as spirits rise like desire.

Each stone speaks in turn
and in chorus—irregular, worn smooth,
swept out and back, heard

and not heard by avocets and gray whales.
My Viking ancestors listened to stones,
felt vibrations travel fault lines

under oceans from a land
that sends tremors up my spine.
I listen through the soles of my feet,

pick up a gray-black stone
marked with white rune-like swirls,
conjure its time forged in fire.

Old Harbinger

I didn't hear the massive branch tear loose
from the pine towering over my house,
didn't see the casualty

until first light—jagged raw edges,
second skin, cambium, and heartwood exposed
under mottled bark. The central limb

angles down unnaturally,
rests now on the low stone wall, extends
over my silent snow-covered lawn.

I imagine the path of the crash
trailing silver in the night sky
a scant three feet from my bedroom window.

What if a gale force had shifted the trajectory my way?
Old harbinger, the injured tree
must be shorn—unbalanced

branches severed, thick rings sliced from the trunk
and carted away before a new storm
can take me down, limbs quaking.

Lucid Dreaming

Viper, raptor, memory loss—
which one is not like the others?
A swamp moccasin dangles
from the falcon's talons
over the abyss of my forgetting
fragments or whole days
and nights dreaming or waking
in dreaming. Ajoya, Opelika,
Sofia, and on to unnamed places
I've traveled in life or in dreams.
Fear rises like mist or
exits stage left, invisible as always.
I inhabit each fear,
show up with talons or fangs,
with the power to change
this trajectory at will.

Late Migration

Vesper sparrows catch the light,
    loose whistles and trills

around the woman in dry grasslands
    who imagines a homeland
she's never seen, surrounded
    by currents upwelling, downwelling,

echoes of a great migration
    of people who became her people.

What did they mean to find, escape,
    create before they laid their burden down,
passed it on, gave it over
    to a daughter, lover, mother, or stranger?

She catches her breath,
    takes wing in morning light.

In Situ

I looked for you in every room,
on each street from Rabat to Dubrovnik.
I tried in vain to catch you through my shadow,
looked the wrong way,
or slept too late to catch the train.
Each night I searched new rooms opening
in that house in the mountains—
inner walls crumbling—white room
filled with morning light, another aura blue.
I looked for you all my life, love,
not knowing I carried you everywhere.

In the Dark in the Light

And the man who can't sleep
And the man who can't wake up
Are the same man.
—Li-young Li

Maybe this time I will stay awake all day,
take in each new green unfolding
on the hillside, each nuance
of your sadness. Maybe this time
I will suspend judgment,
accept the possibility of unseen blooms—
not this or that, love me or leave me,
but stay until a thin moon rises
through leafing trees. After sunset
lights blaze all over the house, spill out
into the night through lucent branches
outside my window and down
the muted street. I flick off the lights,
sit with my usual fear of the unseen,
beneficent or malicious.
I settle like dust, drink in the dark,
feel it enter my skin.

Poem

I circumnavigate on a low tone hummed
          before anyone had words. Rise and fall
like water music. Invincible and fragile as air, I persist
          without yelling and waving my arms.
Yell and wave my arms. Persist in dreams and caravans
          through sand dunes and slums. I grow bored
knowing where to find my slippers by the door.
          Forget the side doors of childhood and remember
them in the middle of the night. Older than anyone
          living, I speak a dead language with the ease
of my mother tongue, remember the taste of jicama
          and cayenne. I have no fear of holding hands
in Kandahar in broad daylight, bear witness
          to the fires of sunrise and sunset all day long.
In grasslands and ocean life, lucid and unseeing, I persist.

First Listening, Finnegans Wake

Wake Finnegans and Swedes, Ghanaians
and Greeks, wake inside and isle side, up and over
the Liffey, the Miss Asippi, waters gloaming,
not knowing the Giant Irish Elk you'll never meet,
the ewe, you steeped in green, yellow, red
as doors basking in a sun-bright noon, agleam
in glory, your daughters blooming, legs spread
over the river, heads thrown back, voices
rising into the clouds in song as if they belonged
to one species that wakes to weep at the long sleep
of the mother and brother who abound in us all
in the telling retelling of lives alight, entwined
ever arcing over faces reflected in the river.

Word People

We whose joy swims in the Adriatic and Goose Pond
     Who juxtapose mango and salt
Who cascade the mountain's steep face and lose our way
     in ravines of silence
We who refuse to take refuge in the idea of fate
     Who fold back on ourselves like mobius strips
Who seek sleep to plunge through dreams
     that might harbor red snakes or crows
Who pry open the jaws of despair and climb out
     Who resist shiny metals that might consume us
Who see words as truth and walk with reverence
     through the forests they illuminate

Intelligent Life

You've always sensed you were at the center.
Since the Big Bang, dark matter has been traveling
the space-time continuum toward you, intelligent life.

For millennia, the serpent has been swallowing its tail
in eternal return while distant galaxies spin away
on paths too huge for humans to grasp.

Faced with infinity, you might choose to lie down
on your couch, like you, composed of tiny particles—
mostly space hurtling through space.

Close-up photos of a star in its death throes
might remind you of the dark that will descend
after your brief days here or of light years from the flash

to the eagle sailing over the village square
as snowmelt flows into the White River toward oceans
alive with species as fragile as your own.

Faced with infinity, significant speck, you might choose
this planet, island, single patch of emerald grass
as the only chance you can count on.

Beyond Five Islands

A pair of osprey nest
at the top of the tallest tree on the island,
water pools in the granite slab
at the ocean's edge, and we drift off
under cotton and down as your watch ticks
on the bureau. I may sleep through
to morning, never knowing
what wild dream carries you.

Minestra Maritata

We stir the married soup
made from broth that's simmered
in your grandmother's iron pot
at the back of the stove for years.
I wield my mother's knife to slice garlic
and red onion. You toss in more peppers,
humming your evening song.
Take it up to a boil and back down
to let the flavors blend.
Your square, scarred hand ladles out
just enough escarole and beef.

Love and Bondage

The clarinet sings off-key, opens the heart space,
    and I slip the bonds of my skin.
Heat sweeps through me like a tidal wave
    when you cross the room. I swallow my fear
but the heart will not stay in place, nerves
    all over the body, its surface too raw to touch.
When will we descend into the far reaches
    if not now—never? We're safe as we will ever be,
earthquake on the way. Out the window,
    dawn breaks like glass. The sacrificial doves
joy and sorrow nest in my hands.
    We all know what we love most will be taken
from us and transformed on the charnel grounds.
    O walk me to my last day
and sweep my closets clean.

Diptych

Night bird stripped of color inside this space machine—
my breath rises, falls, elides amid resonant echoes.
A cool cloud flows into a vein in my left hand.
In the hindsight of my MRI, flesh under fire, I sign on
to an Amazon tribe. Asymmetry of innocents before
and after. My surgeon marks a green line under each
living breast, measures the space nipple to nipple.
Hello, goodbye, left breast, did I ever know you?

Sleep through the sheen and caw of a midflight knife.
Blue out the window when I wake dry-mouthed
and riddled with tubes. Who's that lying in my bed,
vagrant legs splayed? Weeks slide by. The body spits
stitches, drain tubes slip out slick as worms. Pain sparks
my reconstructed breast. I clip back slimy stems of red
and purple freesia past peak on the sill, arrange survivors
in my alabaster vase. Turn off the music and listen.

Scalpel Song

I hum in my sterile packet, steel tip agleam
       in the dark like starlight, clean as a last plea.
Out now, I keen into white light suffusing
       the operating room. Can you hear me
through your Propofol dreams? What did you pray
       on exhale as you sank under?
Sharp as bad news, I don't flinch with pity for the living
       or the dead. I slice into your skin, taste blood
in the first cut, bright red in open air.
       Your flesh falls to either side of my blade.
I bite deep as needed. Your need is deep and wide.
       I follow lines traced on your left breast,
tunnel up to your collarbone, down below
       the inframammary fold. Your face slack,
breast open, you don't see me pare deadly tumors away,
       don't think of the hand that holds me,
fingertips gloved in plastic. If I carve too far,
       blame the hand, caffeine, the surgeon's daydream.
He peels your breast away. You are lucky, lucky
       to have me in his hand. Trust me. I was made
for this salvation job. Sleep your twilight sleep and wake
       amnesic, released. I will be the life of you.

We Pass Like Thieves

We pass in the grocery store, wheeling
     our anonymous carts
We pass invisible as a summer breeze, tubes hidden
     under loose clothes
We pass marked by scars familiar to our lovers
     Like sleepwalkers, our hands graze
the banister on the way downstairs
     We pass like thieves, stealing each day we can
Like the guilty cleared of all charges,
     like innocents falsely accused
We pass for natives, unremarkable, unscathed
     We pass like ghosts of our former selves,
sorrows mingling in the air
     Like snow geese overhead, we sweep north
or south in season
     We pass like comets trailing our cosmic dust

Saving Daylight

Solstice, equinox, it's all the same to me.
In Nome and Tallahassee we all cry *More light!*

I want my lost light back, that light in your eye
like starlight coming at us at a constant rate of speed.

I want my body back, the twenty-year-old one
with a better brain, heart unclenched.

I audition for the part of myself before
my mastectomy and don't get called back.

Blank space in my chest, alive with lack. I carve
a sad face in the pumpkin, light a flame inside.

Creatures of the deep, we navigate
by our own light but don't bank on saving it.

Blaze

On the first anniversary of my mastectomy I examine
        my reconstructed self—scars grown flatter,
coarser skin blended in on the left breast, still strangely
        rounder, higher than the right. Not erotic.
I didn't ask for bigger and better, just close
        to a matching pair. I circle the nipple made
of skin lifted from my back, feel for the lack of feeling
        in this imitation of a body part lost. Remember
I am lucky to be alive. How did I get here? Choose
        whose hands to trust? After the test results
reject the prophylactic double, saline implant,
        breast made of my belly fat. I never saw
Mother's scar, but online photos expose a carnival
        of shapes, stitched flat or reconstructed.
One woman waited ten years to add her nipples
        and aureola tattoos, deciding at sixty-six
she wanted *to go out with both guns blazing.*
        Guns, sex, love, war—who's to say what's folly?
A prosthetic hand reaches for a wig, falsie, codpiece,
        glass eye. Given or grafted, it's all part
of the real. With sleight of hand and scarves askew,
        we play it the best we can. Thanks, Jane, Carmen,
Sybil, Lenore, and women whose names I've forgotten
        or never known. We pave a way, paint it crimson,
send up a flare. Whatever has been taken from us,
        whatever comes next, here's to the glory.

Terra Infirma

A gull's wing tangled in net, stranded
      at high tide. Scavenging, I don't touch it.
No place is safe with the window open,
      screens off, alligators slithering in the yard,
my piece of terra infirma.

 A slow dance opens the heart.
      The hole gapes, widens in the gyre.
Don't sew me up yet. Let me help you
      with the buttons, the zipper. I'm in over my heart,
the moon, my idea of you, our lips electric.

All the women in the exercise room had lost a breast,
      usually the left. We woke to morphine dreams,
dared to touch our incisions.
      The alien reconstruction, warm to the touch,
gives no milk. The glass eye does not see.

I slouch toward the corner store, tubes protruding.
      Each night I take flight, return in time
for toast and eggs. In the dream my tumors grow wild,
      skin bulges over rogue cells, winter coming on,
rain slick as saliva, leaves trapped in ice.

I burn a clean path through. Below,
      cold water, lakebed, the underworld on fire.
Sparks fly from my eyes and mouth,
      the body capacious as stars.
Catch the wheel and spin it into the vast.

About the Author

Carol Westberg's first book of poems, *Slipstream,* was a finalist for the 2011 New Hampshire Literary Award for Outstanding Book of Poetry, and "Map of Uncertain Soundings," within that collection, was a finalist for the Ruth Stone Prize. Born in Berkeley, California, Carol grew up on a farm in Iowa and earned degrees from Duke, Stanford, and Vermont College. She's worked as a teacher, writer, editor, and communications consultant. The parent of two grown daughters, she lives with her husband in Hanover, New Hampshire.

CPSIA information can be obtained at www.ICGtesting.com
Printed in the USA
LVOW11s1642050815

448963LV00003B/709/P